Penny stock

A quick beginner trading guide

By Richard Smiths

Table of Contents

Introduction

I want to thank you and congratulate you for downloading the book, Penny stock.

This book contains proven steps and strategies on how to earn in penny stocks.

Everyone wants to achieve financial freedom. People want a life well-lived without having to worry about money. This can actually be achieved but it takes a lot of discipline and focus. A lot of books and articles have been written about different methods to earn money. This book is one of them.

You'll learn a lot of concepts about penny stocks through this book. Although there are some critics to this type of investment, it isn't necessarily bad if you try to learn about it and decide later if you want to dabble in it. What's important is that you have the willingness to learn about penny stocks.

Many think that it's hard to get a job out there in this market, but the truth of the matter is, it's only hard because you're not looking hard enough. I'm writing this book to show you how to use penny stocks, to give you a simple overview on how it's done, why it works, and how to get started in this type of investment that allows you to attain the financial freedom that you need in life.

Thanks again for downloading this book, I hope you enjoy it!

Chapter 1   What is a Penny Stocks?

Penny stocks originate their name from the very low price per share that these stocks are traded.Buyers might sometimes call them "micro-cap stocks," although this type of stock is more often categorized according to market capitalization that falls between $50 and $300 million.

The Securities and Exchange Commission of the United States defines a penny stock as a security that trades at lowers than $5 a share. They can be dealt at low prices because these are issued by very small companies and are usually quoted over-the counter (OTC) on Pink Sheets or the OTCBB. However, there are exceptions to the rule such as those traded on securities exchanges. On the contrary, large, publicly traded corporations can command high prices per share and can be found quoted on major stock exchanges.

Generally, a growing company, with limited resources and cash, offers a penny stock to investors. The stock generates low trading volumes because investors don't give it much attention. It is often traded on Pink Sheets and Over-the-counter Bulletin Board. A penny stock is a primary target of market manipulations, which can't be used in stocks traded on the stock market. Therefore, investors must exercise caution when trading penny stocks. It is true that these stocks can generate huge returns but it can also bring about huge losses.

A penny stock has the lowest market capitalization. It is usually subject to adjustment and pump in addition to dump scams. It is furthermore highly volatile and presents a lot of risk to buyers. In the Us, the Economic Sector Monitoring Authority and the SEC have rules and rules for you to define and determine its sale.

Penny trading and investing is not pertaining to small time investors several so-called financial experts recommend. This happens because it involves a good understanding of what sort of market moves. And being unable to tell the signals of when to offer or buy more can be quite frustrating. Fortunately, this book will provide you with insights on tips on how to maximize your endeavor into penny stock investment

Chapter 2   Find marketplace and brokers

A penny stock broker facilitates trading by offering the necessary trading platform for investors and merchants. He can also influence the buying and selling patterns, preferences, and behaviors on the stakeholders by offering sales, marketing, as well as recommendations. As these kinds of, it is of importance to a trader or investor to find the right broker for his penny stocks investment.

A lots of these brokers currently provide online as well as mobile trading tools. A dematerialized account is a depository of the investor's shares while nostro is the financial institution account for buying and selling shares. Only a few brokers provide nostro features. Since penny trading is highly assuming in nature, price ranges can fluctuate erratically.

Reliable and instant money transfers are needed for timely as well as efficient trading at desired prices. An investor may well suffer significant losses if you'll find bottlenecks in the transfer of cash. Therefore, it 's best for him to select a broker who provides both nostro as well as depository facilities.

When it comes to penny stocks, transactional costs play an important role. It is important for the investor to learn about transaction prices, which can easily be located on the broker's website. The individual must also take particular discover of additional fine print listed on the website.

Some brokers may charge the very least brokerage fee every share. This signifies that an additional fee per share could possibly be charged to the investor for each and every transaction. For example, a $0. 10 inventory with $0. 03 minimum broker agent fee per share will surely cost about $0. 13 every share. For 10, 000 shares of an penny stock, the investor should pay $300 a lot more than the present market price.

Some brokers can also charge a bare minimum brokerage fee every order. For example, a 1, 000 shares involving penny stock with economy price of $0. 01 and 3% broker agent or $10 bare minimum brokerage fee every trade order will surely cost the investor $10. 30. However, since $0. 30 is lower than $10, the investor should pay the

$10 bare minimum brokerage fee. Thus, he will pay $20 for your transaction.

A broker can also set additional prices for large purchases. This large order surcharge will apply in the event the investor buys shares that happen to be more than the maximum shares set because of the broker.Also the broker can also set monthly bare minimum trades. If an investor doesn't meet the required amount of trades, he could possibly be charged an additional fee.

There can also be an annual preservation fee, which is billed by brokers for each and every trading account. Additional charges can also include fees for cash transfers, depository records, etc. Some brokers also demand a minimum deposit to open a penny stock trading bill. Furthermore, they also fee additional fees for accounts which have been inactive for an extended time. They may also charge a withdrawal fee each time money is transferred in the trading account to the investor's bank.

Now that you might have the basics down and you are mentally prepared to purchase penny stocks, it's time to find where these are listed. The key stock exchanges such as NASDAQ and NYSE accomplish list cheap stocks, but these will not be necessarily considered penny stocks. As previous, these exchanges possess stringent requirements of which companies must fulfill and companies trading penny stocks are simply not around their standards nevertheless. So, penny stocks are traded such as off-exchange, it means that they're dealt without assistance from a stock exchange. Unlike exchange buying and selling, the market prices will not be published and remain involving the two parties engaged inside transaction. This boosts the risks involved in trading.

OTC Markets Class, also known because Pink Sheets, is a listing service that provides market information for OTC securities. Listed companies will not be registered with the SEC and have no minimum needs for trading. The OTC Message Board (OTCBB) can also be used for NON-PRESCRIPTION securities. It offers more transparency in comparison with Pink Sheets, but market capitalization as well as minimum share price will not be required. Companies previously stated on stock exchanges but forget to sustain requirements would often turn out trading on OTCBB.

The best way to trade penny stocks is with an online dealer. It would be good to select brokers who specialize in penny stocks. Take notice that different traders defined a penny stocks differently. Pick brokers who charge a set rate in relation to trade commissions. The reason being the volume is important when trading penny stocks and you don't want to increasingly save money to raise your financial well being. A per-share agreement becomes very limiting over time. Also, be wary of any fees how the broker will fee and for whichever reasons. You are able to trade an unlimited amount of shares without having to pay extra. Understand any different special terms how the broker imposes in clients so you don't get surprised simply by rules and limits.

As with every other business, customer services important. Friendly, thorough and easily accessible support can make yourself easier you probably have any issues or inquiries. Some brokers may also be more generous than others in relation to sharing market data and research. A broker who sends alerts for stocks to exchange would be very useful in helping you navigate the market.

Some brokers have a tendency to limit choices according to the price per write about or other attributes. Their digital trading platform should have an easy-to-navigate user interface that you can understand. Find out if they have support for all you devices such while laptops, tablets and smartphones and your OS of choice as well as other system requirements.

As a result of price volatility of penny stocks, the hold time on the phone and the response time on the website are prime considerations. An investor has to enter or depart a position instantly because prices can change quickly. If they needs different purchaser services like stories and research tools, technical indicators, as well as data feeds, it is vital that he consult his broker regarding their costs because most of these services are offered for a high fee.

How to invest in penny stocks

Open up a Trading Bank account

When an entrepreneur opens a buying and selling account, he must consider support services, fees, and how quickly funds is usually transferred. There are stockbrokers with various specializations so it will be best for him to buy around for a free account which matches their requirements.

A penny stock investor should be very concerned in regards to the broker's fee construction. There are stockbrokers who charge profits per share, that is a scheme with a set rate for the very least number of shares. They also fee another rate for succeeding shares. This fee structure is designed for an investor who has low capital. Regarding penny stock merchants, it is more cost-effective to search for a broker who gives a low flat pace per transaction. Having a low fee, the trader can generate a higher price because of much less commissions and costs.

Chapter 3   How to Choose the Right Penny Stock

Not all stocks listed about the OTCBB will get listed into a major stock trade. Most companies will likely be bankrupt or fade into oblivion also before they benefit from their products and services. However, the trading volume of OTCBB still remains its phenomenal progress. About 650 billion shares happen to be traded in 2006. majority penny stock companies haven't any revenue.However, it is easy for traders to be able to choose a company which will probably succeed.

The first place where one can look into when judging the soundness of purchasing a penny stock would be the financial statements from the company. Seeing high debt and low sales just isn't necessarily a red flag because a lot of startup companies do begin the life cycle this method. Losses are expected at the start with positive income finally coming in perhaps by another financial year. These businesses are not instantly busts. Take a peek at the business that the company is operating in. Is it an emerging specialized niche? Does the item have promise in the years to come? Do your research and find out what the experts assert about the companies engaged inside a similar area. In recent many years, tech startups have become a dime a dozen. But, there are those that really offer revolutionary I. T. remedies that consumers react positively to. Often, a product may be quite in advance of its time similar to the predecessor of this Apple MacBook laptop computers. The big, clunky laptops were fun and stylish, but during the time, people were still observing their way around desktop PCs. A few decades after, MacBook have become the benchmark inside laptop design and quality. Learn to realize potential before all others does.

Also, keep abreast associated with rumors of mergers and acquisitions that smaller companies are inclined to. These usually create a beneficial rise inside stock prices, especially if at all the latter. Either way, the news will create interest in the stocks, so you'll want to monitor any developments so you will know how to proceed with the stocks that you're holding. Young companies at the start of their life cycle is definitely the ones that would experience sudden growths. This tapers away or plateaus since the company matures and stock prices stabilize. Thus, the beginning is an excellent time to start buying the company. You can find that penny stocks could multiply in value in a mere a matter associated with hours. Understand in which the company is inside its life never-ending cycle. If it already quite after dark infancy stage but still has very reduced share prices, then there can be something inherently wrong with all the way it is progressing business and you ought to no longer be waiting for some time when the stocks would suddenly rise in value.

Creating Probability Work

A penny stock investor must know what sort of company he's seeking. In addition, he must also possess the appropriate tools to assist him look to find the best stock. Since the average price of a cent stock is $0. 10, will probably be best to seek out stocks priced involving $0. 05 and $2. If the investor wants to search for a higher-priced any amount of money stock, he could find fewer stocks.

He must seek out penny stocks with at the very least 100, 000 stocks of average everyday volume. The focus have to be on those stocks which are on an uptrend. Thus, the trader can use the positive 3-week and 10-week price information, and with this 9-day simple moving average in excess of its 18-day opposite number. The trader can easily exclude companies having negative earnings progress rates or damaging earnings per discuss. He must concentrate on stocks on a good uptrend for at the very least a 5-day time period. He must be thinking about stocks which are often on an uptrend.

Each penny stock must pass what is this great, short interest, and visual tests. A wholesome chart pattern becomes necessary. It must show that the price is when using uptrend and going above the assist levels. To pass what is this great test, the penny stock company must create positive news so as to attract more traders. A short interest is often a percentage of the whole shares which was sold short yet hadn't been closed yet. If this percentage is higher than 5%, it can mean trouble. However, if this percentage continues to increase, it will push the cost even higher.

Selecting the Winners

A retail trader may commit one of his biggest exchanging mistakes if he sees a cent stock as something is affordable. He believes that he will bring in more cash if he tends to buy more shares of one penny stock as an alternative to buying shares of the higher-priced stock listed on a major exchange. Although it may look rational, it is important that he doesn't overlook the number of shares outstanding.

For instance, companies A and B have $100, 000, 000 industry capitalization each. Should the share price associated with company A can be $0. 10, it indicates that its amount of shares outstanding is add up to 1, 000, 000, 000. In contrast, if company B's discuss price is $100, its amount of shares outstanding can be 1, 000, 000. Thus, before company Some sort of gets fully capitalized, it requires investors to purchase the 1, 000, 000, 000 stocks. It is simpler to sell 1, 000, 000 stocks at $100 as compared to 1, 000, 000, 000 stocks at $0. 10.

An investor must also be familiar with dilution of penny stocks. This means a stock's number associated with shares outstanding may grow uncontrollable by using employee investment, stock splits, and share issuance to improve capitalization. If the business issues more stocks, ownership percentage of investors will likely be diluted. Therefore, if an investor wants to achieve success in penny stocks, he must have the ability to search for a company that includes a very strong share structure making sure that existing owners won't view the value of their own investment eroded through continuous dilution

Spotting the most beneficial Penny Stock

Cent stock companies include low market capitalization. Everyone, who wants to invest in them, must take into account the fundamentals of these firms. He must find out about their share composition, competition, and underlying fundamentals making sure that he'll have the ability to determine the most effective stock to invest in.

The investor should also know the areas where these penny stocks belong. Most penny stocks are in this mining and alloys sector.

Aggressive inducement plans, increased opposition, and fund operations have to be considered if he wants to earn more revenue from these penny stocks.

Using Financial Ratios to determine the Winning Stock

If a any amount of money stock company has the capacity to provide adequate monetary disclosure, the investor are capable of doing analysis to determine if at all worth investing in it. If there's having a positive trend and strong numbers about the financial statements, he will be able to foretell the future expectations of performance from the penny stock business.

The Liquidity ratios

These ratios are widely-used to compute for penny stocks since many are unable to afford their short-term debt. If the liquidity relation is low, it indicates that the any amount of money stock company can be advancing its procedures or struggling to remain in business.

The particular Leverage Ratios

Leverage ratios resemble liquidity ratios. Both of them concentrate on the ability from the penny stock company to its debts. Nevertheless, with leverage ratios, the concern can be on long-term credit card debt.

The Performance Percentage

The performance relation quantifies the revenues generated by the company through the income statement. It's important for a any amount of money stock company showing consistent earnings progress.

The Valuation Ratios

Valuation ratios measure the penny stock's attractiveness at its existing price. In common, it is easy for a penny stock to become significantly overvalued. An investor can use these ratios as tools to determine if a certain stock is overvalued or even undervalued.

Chapter 4   Advice for Penny Stock Trading

Penny stocks are very susceptible to fraud and hoaxes. Trading penny stocks is definitely not for the actual faint of heart. The high risks that come with very volatile stocks might cause many less seasoned traders to forfeit their cool and panic once values commence to plummet. But, that is the nature of penny stocks. As with any other kind of stock, time should be working for you. Patience is key to investing. Here you can easily see some advice for you if you wish to start penny trading.

Learn to recognize the real superstars among the actual wannabes. Do not get attached to any one company for sentimental (It was my first deal!), emotional (It is run by way of nice old n lady!) or maybe truly irrational (I likes their gooseberry jam that nobody different likes!) reason. Drop the within performing stocks if it is time and keep the good ones providing it still makes sense for this. Always have the mindset of a businessman who can abandon a settling ship when it becomes sure it will only bring about more losses. Remember that you have no obligation to be faithful to a new company's stock, no matter the amount personal or relational investment you may have with it. Your financial investment must always reign supreme.

Follow the best rule of financial, which is diversification. Simply put: usually do not put all your eggs in a single basket. When a single spoils, it affects the others and you lose all of your eggs. Thus, place your money in various kinds of investments instead of placing all of your money in just one. Do not hope that one company's penny stocks is likely to make you rich. That may be increasing risk in an already risky circumstance. Likewise, do not only invest in penny stocks, but also recognize less volatile blue penny stocks coming from large corporations using a long history connected with excellent business performance and good predictions. Furthermore, do not only invest in stocks and options, but also consider bonds, real house, and even gold bars. Investing in penny stocks takes a great deal of commitment because these people move so rapidly. Daily monitoring of your stocks is critical. Letting your stocks sit for an extended time without trading is just not ideal. Learn to adapt to changing market environments to maximize your earnings.

Monitor the price Up and down of Some Penny Stocks

Because a trader can buy a sizable volume of shares, he can crank out large profits if you take advantages of every day changes in the price of the penny stock. In addition, by using short-term strategies, the investor has to cope with lesser risks.

Avoid the Hype

A lot connected with penny stock companies are doing artificial methods to increase the value of their stock by enticing inexperienced investor to purchase them by buying shares of stock. Because more buyers are receiving into the penny stock, it is actually expected that it is price will substantially increase. This is rooked by unscrupulous folks and businesses by selling their particular shares for a higher price. Thus, traders really should make a thorough research firstly the business before buying it. The historical price fluctuations is usually analyzed and economic news works extremely well in order to gauge when the penny stock is a superb investment or not.

Use Effective Techniques

To maximize gains and mitigate risk, an individual can certainly trade consistently just one stock and remember to research about the actual company's business. He can learn quickly and with assurance predict any transform in value by using effective strategies. A lot of penny stock companies have small-scale businesses and generate lower revenues monthly. These enterprises can easily collapse. As this kind of, it is better to select a penny stock company using a broad customer base. The investor can also choose a company which is in to high-demand product or service and service growth.

Analyze Volume

In choosing the penny stock, the trader must pick a business which offers high amount of shares. Top penny stocks works extremely well for day buying and selling activities if these types of stocks have 1000 of shares at a low price. The person can purchase and sell these stocks often for short amounts of time in order to be able to earn more gains. However, it's important to discover if there is a lot of investors and traders who definitely are interested in buying and selling the shares of this company. If we have a high demand to get a particular penny stock, the shares can certainly generate substantial gains. By analyzing the actual trading volume, a trader can pick the right penny stocks for his day trading investing strategies.

Take Benefit of Volatility

A lot of investors can preserve shares of stock for so many years before locking of their profits by seling them. Within this long time frame, the company sells all its assets, be merged having another company, or go out of business. On another hand, top penny stocks, which are additional volatile, can be ordered by traders and sold before the trading day finishes. The volatility of penny stocks ensures that the actual traders sell their shares inside day so that you can maximize the short-term gains.

Buy The Shares Of Stock At The Appropriate Time

If there's a new sharp drop inside value of a penny stock, a lot connected with its shareholders will want to sell their explains to you. Therefore, a large amount of the stock is available for purchase at a good deal. Once the explains to you are bought, it really is imperative for the actual trader to keep track of the fluctuations of the price until this tops its typical daily peak next the shares can always be sold for greatest profit.

Chapter 5 Why Investors Need To Be Worried

A penny stock, especially one that trades below $0. 01, is usually thinly traded.

Manipulators and stock promoters often utilize it for its water pump and dump structure. They initially buy the majority of this stock after that inflate its talk about price through misleading and false claims.

A pump along with dump scheme is fraudulent. Some organizations or individuals invest in penny stock explains to you and use mail blasts, fake pr releases, stock message snowboards, chat rooms, and websites to build interest to your stock. In most cases, a person will claim undertake a hot tip about a particular penny stock so that you can persuade naive investors to acquire the shares swiftly. When more investors find the shares, the price will skyrocket to entice more investors to purchase the shares. Finally, the manipulators will sell their shares and generate huge profits there.

For example, rapper 50 Dollar used Twitter to help dramatically increase the price tag on HNHI, a penny stock. He owned thirty million shares and was able to earn $8. 7 million through the sale. Another example could be the case of Lithium Seek Group whose current market capitalization went approximately at least $350 million following company executed a comprehensive mail campaign. In the 10-Q form the organization filed on December 31, 2010, it listed the firm with no assets and absolutely nothing revenues. After your promotion, it bought lithium exploration properties to cope with the concerns of the press.

In a number of cases, a company are capable of doing a pump along with dump when it desires to promote its stock. In general, the price tag on the penny stock moves because of momentum. It is volatile with the spread and the way the Securities and Exchange Commission regulates the idea. The SEC can halt the exchanging when it updates that its price went up very rapid. Until such time that it is released by SECURITIES AND EXCHANGE COMMISSION'S again, the price of the penny can move either way and investors don't have got control over their shares.

Regulating the Trade of penny stocks

In the United states of america, a penny stock must meet different standards like minimum shareholder equity, current market capitalization, and price tag. A publicly-listed stock, which is dealt around the stock exchange, just isn't controlled like a penny stock even although its price is below $5. It really is classified as some sort of low-priced stock and not as a any penny stock. The Financial Marketplace Regulatory Authority and also the Securities and Exchange Commission control penny stock trading through their rules and regulations. The State regarding Georgia was the very first to enact a wide penny stock legislation. After the legislation was upheld by the US District The courtroom, the SEC and also the FINRA made comprehensive revisions on their regulations, which had been effective in confining or closing traders and brokers. Even so, pump and dispose of schemes by unregistered individuals and groups never have been addressed by simply these regulations.

Understanding the Risk

A penny stock can be quite volatile. Putting money from it may result to help substantial gains but we have a greater probability of experiencing losses. As this sort of, it is important for any investor to watch out for trading penny futures. Money managers, common funds, and index finances have set rules to visit so they can't trade penny stocks. Therefore, only several investors place their money in penny stocks. It is important to note that the issue of liquidity can't end up being ignored. A retail investor may get stuck with a penny stock for an extended time if there is not enough supply and demand for him to trade his stock.

Chapter 6   The Risks and Potential

Investing penny stocks can be be extremely risky but it also has a great potential to get significant returns. On the other hand, it must be noted large amounts of people gamble on penny stocks and significant returns could be generated over the short term. A lot connected with companies offering penny stocks are usually more than leveraged or headed towards bankruptcy. Some corporations are furthermore shell companies that scammers use to dupe people.

The Risks Of Penny stocks Trading

In nearly all cases, penny stocks are traded on Over-the-counter Bulletin Table or Pink Bed sheets. An investor will find challenging looking for information about companies offering their stocks around the OTCBB so he will find it hard to make a logical conclusion of a particular company. Additionally, for both Pink Sheets and OTCBB, we have a lack of trustworthy sources about these stocks. In simple fact, listing on sometimes exchange doesn't even call for a company to fulfill some minimum expectations.

Furthermore, there is a lot of liquidity in trading penny stocks. It may be possible to get a penny stock but disposing the actual shares will pose a problem because the trading volume can be quite low. This means the investor will find it hard to sell his penny stock even when he wants to lock in his profits because you will discover fewer interested buyers on the target price. The investor will likely then have to watch for a willing customer or sell the stock at the lower price. When the person decides to wait, he may find himself trapped in a very pump-and dump plan and sees even his capital being erased. If he decides to reduce the price, he will see a reduction in his profits.

Finally, there are a great number of scammers offering biased tips about a particular penny stock. A likely investor may obtain brochures through electronic mail or snail postal mail. The material, usually contains a number of hyped-up claims the specific penny inventory will experience significant gains as a result of revolutionary technology. The unsuspecting individual doesn't understand that the person or even company sending the brochures is selling his individual shares at discounted prices.

Penny Stock Scams

A penny Stock can pose problems not simply to the individual, but to the actual Securities and Exchange Commission likewise. Its poor liquidity and lack of information make it a simple target for scammers.

Some penny Stock companies pay individuals to recommend the actual stock using several media like radio stations shows, newsletters, and also financial television. An investor may be given a spam email informing him of an great earning chance. It is best for your person to check should the people recommending the stock are being paid for his or her services.

It is usually possible for an investor to be scammed by offshore brokers. The SEC allows companies to sell stocks to overseas investors offshore with no need to register the actual stocks. What these businesses do is which they sell their explains to you of stock at the discount to overseas buyers, who then sell them returning to investors in the United states of America at the higher price. These offshore brokerages often make cold calls to potential investors and give hot tips to entice those to buy the inventory.

Avoid Getting scammed

Most penny stock companies advertise through e-mail spam. Similar to spam, these emails contain success stories of which purport " I managed to get $1, 000 richer everyday! " and stories that confess " My spouse and i was skeptical in the beginning, but I feel now a believer throughout Company X!. Penny stocks should be consumed seriously. It isn't as simple as choosing a magic bean and also watching it grow right beanstalk that contains money

Jordan Belfort with the Wolf of Walls Street fame after said about options trading, " As long as it gets done, the item doesn't matter just how. " Lying, cheating and crime are typical fair game to be able to brokers and companies that are set on making bank on the expense of naive investors. A common myth that is spread to likely investors is of which Walmart stocks was previously penny stocks. That is untrue. The source of the misunderstanding is based on their split-adjusted price during which adjustments were done for their historic stock prices despite the fact that they were by no means traded at any amount of money stock prices. Walmart did start off trading OTC for a couple years just before being eventually listed around the NYSE. A identical story has spread about

Microsoft, but stock splits are once again the reason for the sub-$1 costs.

When doing pursuit, it is sometimes better to disregard any information willingly provided by management. They will declare and do anything that you buy their stocks. They will help to make false promises and also downplay existing issues within their organizations. It is the most suitable to do your own personal independent research or count on information provided by credible vacation sources. Also, steer clear of promotional resources, press releases along with other media and promoting presence, because they come directly through the companies themselves and can easily be misrepresented.

Finally, never pay for information. Find bloggers whom give advice and tricks for free to his or her readers. Join online groups that discuss very cheap stocks and provide you with up-to date news around the markets. Books, fund journals, newspapers and periodicals should publish additional legitimate information rather than online sources that not go through editorial reviews or even expert criticism.

Buying stocks is any high-stakes game, but this is a game that ought to be played strategically along with the proper way of thinking lest one declines victim to dishonest those who only want to exploit people who are blinded with the promise of easy money through penny stocks.

Why Is A Penny Stock A Risky Investment?

First, the public doesn't have a access to just about all information. To be successful in investing, an investor need to have enough tangible information to assist him make a fantastic decision. Those companies listed on Pink Linens don't file with SEC in order that they aren't regulated or perhaps scrutinized publicly. Moreover, more information about they then isn't credible.

Next, Pink Sheets along with Over-the-counter Bulletin Table don't require companies to fulfill some minimum standard requirements. It may be possible for a company to become listed on these exchanges since it failed to keep its position about the major exchange. The OTCBB calls for listed companies to at the very least file SEC documents regularly. However, Pink Linens doesn't have just about any requirement.

Third, the majority of listed companies within OTCBB and Pink Sheets are both nearing bankruptcy or perhaps newly created. Thus, these companies could possibly have no track record by any means. It is very difficult to determine the potential of anything stock if the company doesn't have famous information.

Fourth, penny stocks have liquidity issues. It is possible that the investor won't be able to dispose his stock options because he can't find a willing buyer correctly. He may even have to lower his cost if he desires to sell it quickly. Furthermore, some unscrupulous men and women and companies may manipulate the price of a penny stock options through pump along with dump scheme.

This Potential Of Penny Stock

To make money with penny stocks, an individual must get along with the pump-and get rid of scheme. This means which he buys the stock options when he will get the spam email or spam then wait with the other people to purchase it also in order that the trading volume is going to be increased. However, the investor should sell his stocks quickly to freeze his small gains. Timing is crucial with such a strategy. If he misses your initial surge in exchanging volume, he may eventually lose just about all his capital.

Another strategy is to list all penny stocks and perform required research on companies that are fitted with generated revenues, made available liquid stocks, and operated the best website with firm images and get in touch with information. In supplement, these companies need to have a strong stability sheet or is actually debt-free, and include reduced losses or perhaps remained profitable

The Fallacy On the Penny Stock

Unsuspecting investors are made to believe that a lot of currently popular stocks began as penny stock. They believed in which today's large businesses only appreciated within values. By performing required research, an investor will be aware that companies like Wal-Mart and Microsoft had been reduced to pennies as a consequence of stock splits. They then didn't start their businesses at the low market cost.

Lastly, a lot of investors become attracted to penny stocks since they believe that these kinds of stocks will appreciate and give more opportunities. For instance, a $0. 10 reveal price, which likes to $0. 15, has made a 50%

earnings. Therefore, a $1, 000 investment has the capacity to buy 10, 000 shares along with earns $500 after the increase in price. Investors fail to realize that if it's probable to earn $500 from your transaction, it is also possible to reduce $500 or the many capital.

Conclusion

Thank you again for downloading this book!

I hope this book was able to help you to understand and get started on trading penny stocks.

Finally, if you enjoyed this book, then I'd like to ask you for a favor, would you be kind enough to leave a review for this book on Amazon? It'd be greatly appreciated!

Thank you and good luck!

www.ingramcontent.com/pod-product-compliance
Lightning Source LLC
Chambersburg PA
CBHW070743180526
45168CB00004B/1513